5 Minute BIBLE REFLECTIONS for When Life Feels Loud

FOR TEENAGE GIRLS

A 90-Day 5-Minute Bible Devotional to Help Teen Girls Tune Out the Noise and Hear God's Voice

DOROTHY ASTER

"For we are God's masterpiece. He has created us anew in Christ Jesus, so we can do the good things he planned for us long ago."

Ephesians 2:10

DEVOTION

Embracing your authentic identity is the first step towards empowering others to do the same.

REFLECTION

What makes you feel most like yourself? Is it when you're engaging with friends, pursuing a passion, or simply enjoying some quiet time? Take a moment to reflect on these feelings and how they shape your identity.

____

____

____

____

PRAYER

Dear God, as I journey through this life, help me embrace who You created me to be. Remind me of my unique gifts and strengths, and let my heart find peace in my true identity.

You are beautifully unique, a masterpiece crafted by love.

Philippians 4:6–7 reminds us to approach God with our worries and prayers, promising that His peace will guard our hearts and minds. In our most chaotic moments, He invites us to seek solace in prayer, drawing us closer to His comforting presence.

DEVOTION

In prayer, we find a refuge that transforms our worries into peace, teaching us to trust in God's guidance and presence.

REFLECTION

What does prayer mean to you in your daily life? How does it help you navigate your challenges and joys?

____

____

____

____

PRAYER

Dear God, thank you for being a constant presence in our lives. Help us to remember that through prayer, we can always find comfort and strength. May we trust in your love as we lift our hearts to you each day.

Prayer is not just a moment; it's a heartbeat that connects us to our Creator.

NAVIGATING FRIENDSHIPS

"As iron sharpens iron, so one person sharpens another."

Proverbs 27:17

DEVOTION

Navigating friendships is about seeking connections that enrich your soul rather than simply fulfilling social needs.

REFLECTION

What types of friendships bring you joy, and which ones leave you feeling uncertain or drained? Take a moment to think about how each relationship impacts your life and your heart.

____

____

____

____

PRAYER

Dear God, thank you for the gift of friendship. Help me discern which relationships nurture my spirit and guide me in building connections that reflect Your love.

True friendships are like mirrors, reflecting the beauty and authenticity within us.

DEALING WITH PEER PRESSURE

"My daughter, if sinners entice you, do not consent."

Proverbs 1:10

DEVOTION

Stay grounded in your values and remember: true friends will respect you for not succumbing to pressures that don't align with who you are.

REFLECTION

What are some situations in your life where you've felt pressured to go along with what others were doing, even if it didn't feel right to you? How did you handle those moments?

____

____

____

____

PRAYER

Dear Lord, help me to find strength in you when I'm faced with peer pressure. Guide me to make choices that reflect my true self and your love. Surround me with supportive friends who uplift me in my journey.

True strength comes from staying true to yourself, even when it's hard.

Psalm 139:14 reminds us that we are "fearfully and wonderfully made."

DEVOTION

True confidence comes from knowing you are valued and loved just as you are.

REFLECTION

What does confidence look like for you, and in what areas of your life do you feel the most unsure? How might taking small steps to embrace who you are help build your confidence?

____

____

____

____

PRAYER

Dear God, thank you for reminding us that we are wonderfully made. Help us to see ourselves through Your eyes and to embrace our uniqueness with boldness. Fill our hearts with confidence to pursue the passions You've placed within us.

Confidence is not about being perfect; it's about embracing your unique journey.

"Anxiety weighs down the heart, but a kind word cheers it up."

Proverbs 12:25

DEVOTION

In moments of anxiety, remember that vulnerability can lead to strength and healing.

REFLECTION

What anxieties have been creeping into your thoughts lately, and how can you remind yourself of the strength you have within to face them?

____

____

____

____

PRAYER

Dear God, help me to trust in Your peace when anxiety tries to overwhelm me. Teach me to lean on Your strength and know that I am never alone in my struggles. Thank You for being my refuge and guide.

Strength isn't the absence of fear; it's the courage to walk through it.

BALANCING LIFE AND FAITH

"I can do all things through Christ who strengthens me."

Philippians 4:13

DEVOTION

When you nurture your spiritual life, it doesn't just balance your daily tasks; it enriches your entire experience.

REFLECTION

What does it look like for you to balance your daily life with your faith? Consider the choices you make each day—how can you invite God into those moments?

____

____

____

____

PRAYER

Dear God, help me find harmony in my life and faith. Teach me to lean on You in every situation and remind me of Your presence in my daily activities.

Faith is not just a part of life; it's the best guide for living it fully.

DISCOVERING YOUR PASSION

"Delight yourself in the Lord, and He will give you the desires of your heart."

Psalm 37:4

DEVOTION

In the quest of discovering your passion, remember that the journey is just as valuable as the destination, allowing your heart to bloom in unexpected directions.

REFLECTION

What activities make you feel most alive? When do you lose track of time and feel a sense of joy? Reflect on these moments and consider how they might guide you toward discovering your passion.

____

____

____

____

PRAYER

Dear God, help me to uncover the passions you've woven into my heart. Grant me the courage to explore and embrace what brings me joy, leading me closer to my true self.

Your passions are the whispers of your soul, revealing the unique path meant just for you.

"For I am convinced that neither death nor life, neither angels nor demons, neither the present nor the future, nor any powers, neither height nor depth, nor anything else in all creation, will be able to separate us from the love of God that is in Christ Jesus our Lord."

Romans 8:38–39

DEVOTION

In moments of doubt or loneliness, remember that God's love embraces you without conditions—allow this truth to anchor your identity and empower your journey.

REFLECTION

What does it mean to you to know that God loves you no matter what you do or how you feel? Can you think of a time when you felt unlovable, but somehow still sensed His love?

____

____

____

____

PRAYER

Dear God, thank you for loving me without conditions or limits. Help me to feel and embrace that love every single day, so I can share it with others.

God's love is a constant light, shining even through our darkest days.

"For where two or three gather in my name, there am I with them."

Matthew 18:20

DEVOTION

True community teaches us that together, we can embark on a journey of growth and understanding, making life's challenges feel lighter and victories sweeter.

REFLECTION

What does community mean to you, and how do the people in your life shape who you are becoming? How can you deepen these relationships or invite new ones into your life?

____

____

____

____

PRAYER

Dear God, thank You for the gift of community in our lives. Help us to embrace our friendships and support each other, reminding us that we are never alone in our journey. May we shine Your light in the lives of those around us.

Together, we are stronger, braver, and more beautiful than we can ever be alone.

"Trust in the LORD with all your heart and lean not on your own understanding; in all your ways submit to him, and he will make your paths straight."

Proverbs 3:5–6

DEVOTION

Embracing change can be daunting, but it often leads to unexpected blessings and growth in our lives.

REFLECTION

What changes are you currently facing in your life, and how do you feel about them? Can you identify a positive outcome that could arise from this transition?

____

____

____

____

PRAYER

Dear God, help me to be brave and open-hearted as I navigate the changes in my life. Grant me the wisdom to see your purpose in every shift and turn. Amen.

Change is the bridge that carries us toward growth and new opportunities.

"Everyone who is called by my name, whom I created for my glory, whom I formed and made."

Isaiah 43:7

DEVOTION

True fulfillment comes not from fitting into others' expectations but from embracing the unique purpose you were created for.

REFLECTION

What does it mean for you to live with purpose in your everyday life? How can you start to align your daily actions with your deepest values?

____

____

____

____

PRAYER

Dear God, help me to see the purpose you have woven into my life. Guide me to make choices that reflect my true self and inspire others along the way. Amen.

Your unique gifts and passions are the tools God has given you to paint the world with your purpose.

James 2:14–17 reminds us that faith without action is empty; if someone is in need and we merely offer good wishes without helping them, what good is that?

DEVOTION

A simple act of kindness can change someone's day—and perhaps even their life—reminding us that our actions have the power to uplift and inspire.

REFLECTION

What acts of kindness have you witnessed or experienced recently that made you feel appreciated or loved? How can you be that source of kindness for someone else today?

____

____

____

____

PRAYER

Dear Lord, thank you for the gift of kindness and the way it brightens our days. Help me to see the opportunities to share love and kindness with those around me. Amen.

Kindness is a language the deaf can hear and the blind can see.

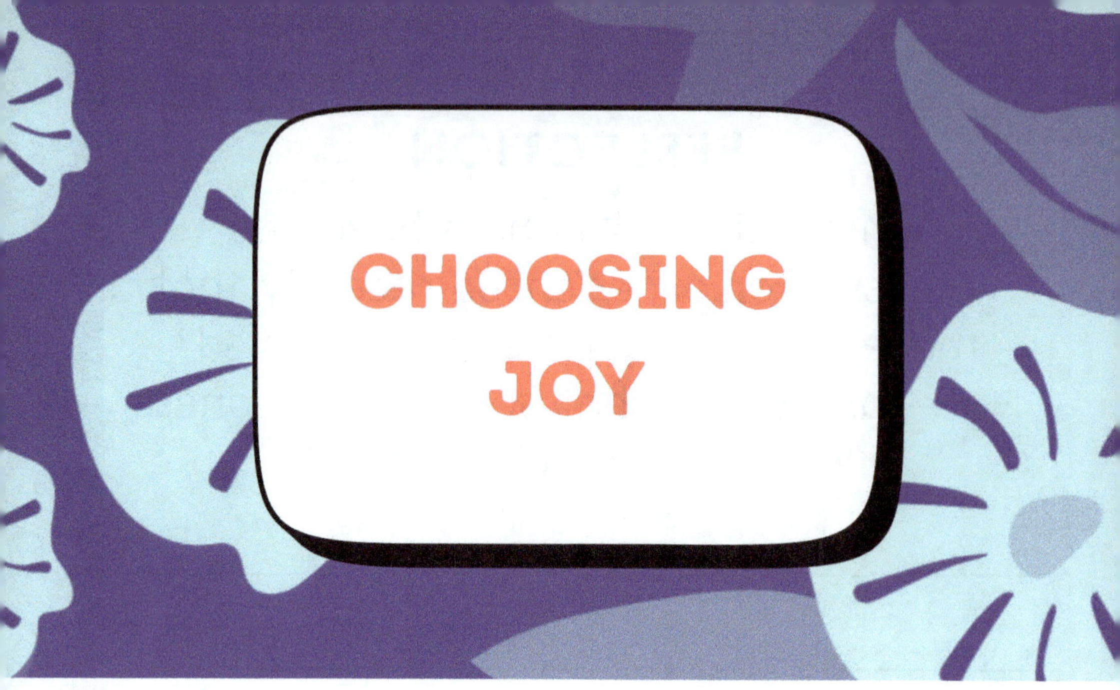

"This is the day that the Lord has made; let us rejoice and be glad in it."

Psalm 118:24

DEVOTION

Every day holds the potential for joy; it requires us to actively seek it out, especially when life feels challenging.

REFLECTION

What brings you joy in your everyday life, and how can you choose to focus on those moments more intentionally this week?

____

____

____

____

PRAYER

Dear God, help me to see the joy that surrounds me each day and give me the strength to choose gratitude, even in challenging times. Fill my heart with your light, so I can share it with others.

Joy is not just a feeling; it's a choice we make to embrace life's moments with gratitude.

"Charm is deceptive, and beauty is fleeting; but a woman who fears the Lord is to be praised."

Proverbs 31:30

DEVOTION

It's essential to remember that your worth is not defined by external appearances but by your character and the love you embrace within.

REFLECTION

What insecurities are you holding onto
right now, and how do they affect the
way you see yourself and connect with
others?

____

____

____

____

PRAYER

Dear God, help me to see myself
through Your eyes. Give me the courage
to face my insecurities and remind me
of the beautiful qualities You've placed
in me. Amen.

*Your worth is not defined by
your insecurities, but by the
love that surrounds you.*

"The Spirit of the Lord will rest on him —the Spirit of wisdom and of understanding, the Spirit of counsel and of might, the Spirit of knowledge and of the fear of the Lord."

Isaiah 11:2

DEVOTION

Embrace your gifts, for they are the unique threads woven into the tapestry of your life, meant to uplift not only yourself but those around you.

REFLECTION

What unique talents or passions do you feel drawn to that might be part of your spiritual gifts? How can you explore these interests further to understand how they can serve others and bring joy to your life?

____

____

____

____

PRAYER

Dear God, thank you for the unique gifts you've placed within each of us. Help me to discover and embrace my spiritual gifts, using them to grow closer to you and uplift those around me.

Your spiritual gifts are like stars in the night sky, waiting to shine brightly and guide others along their journeys.

"So that you may become blameless and pure, children of God without fault in a warped and crooked generation. Then you will shine among them like stars in the sky."

Philippians 2:15

DEVOTION

In times when life feels challenging or overwhelming, remember that even the smallest actions can create ripples of light that brighten someone else's path.

REFLECTION

What does it mean for you to be a light in the world around you, and how can you reflect that light in your everyday life?

____

____

____

____

PRAYER

Dear God, thank you for the gift of your light within us. Help us to share that light with others, especially in moments when it feels difficult or dark. Guide us to be beacons of hope and love in our communities.

Your light doesn't just brighten your path; it illuminates the way for others.

"Bear with each other and forgive one another if any of you has a grievance against someone. Forgive as the Lord forgave you."

Colossians 3:13

DEVOTION

Forgiveness is not just about letting go; it's a brave choice to choose connection over conflict, nurturing our hearts in love.

REFLECTION

What does forgiveness mean to you, and how can letting go of past hurt free you to embrace joy in your life today?

____

____

____

____

PRAYER

Dear God, thank You for Your endless grace and the power of forgiveness. Help me to release any grudges I hold and to fill my heart with love and compassion, just as You have shown me.

Forgiveness is not just a gift we give to others but a freedom we allow ourselves to embrace.

"Above all else, guard your heart, for everything you do flows from it."

Proverbs 4:23

DEVOTION

Learning the art of setting boundaries allows you to preserve your energy and create space for what truly matters, enriching both your life and relationships.

REFLECTION

What does setting a personal boundary mean to you, and how might it change the way you interact with your family, friends, and yourself? Are there areas in your life where you feel you need to say "no" to something that doesn't serve you well?

____

____

____

____

PRAYER

Dear God, thank you for helping me understand the importance of boundaries in my life. Help me to be brave and wise in setting them, so I can honor myself and others better each day. Amen.

Boundaries are not walls; they are fences that protect my peace and well-being.

"The fear of the Lord leads to life, and whoever has it rests satisfied; he will not be touched by harm."

Proverbs 19:23

DEVOTION

Finding rest in God means stepping away from the hustle and allowing His grace to renew our weary souls.

REFLECTION

What does finding rest in God look like for you in your busy life? Take a moment to consider the things that overwhelm you and how resting in Him might bring you peace.

____

____

____

____

PRAYER

Dear God, help me to trust in Your peace as I navigate my daily challenges. Teach me how to find my rest in You, and fill my heart with Your calmness today.

Rest is not just the absence of activity; it's an invitation to be refreshed in His presence.

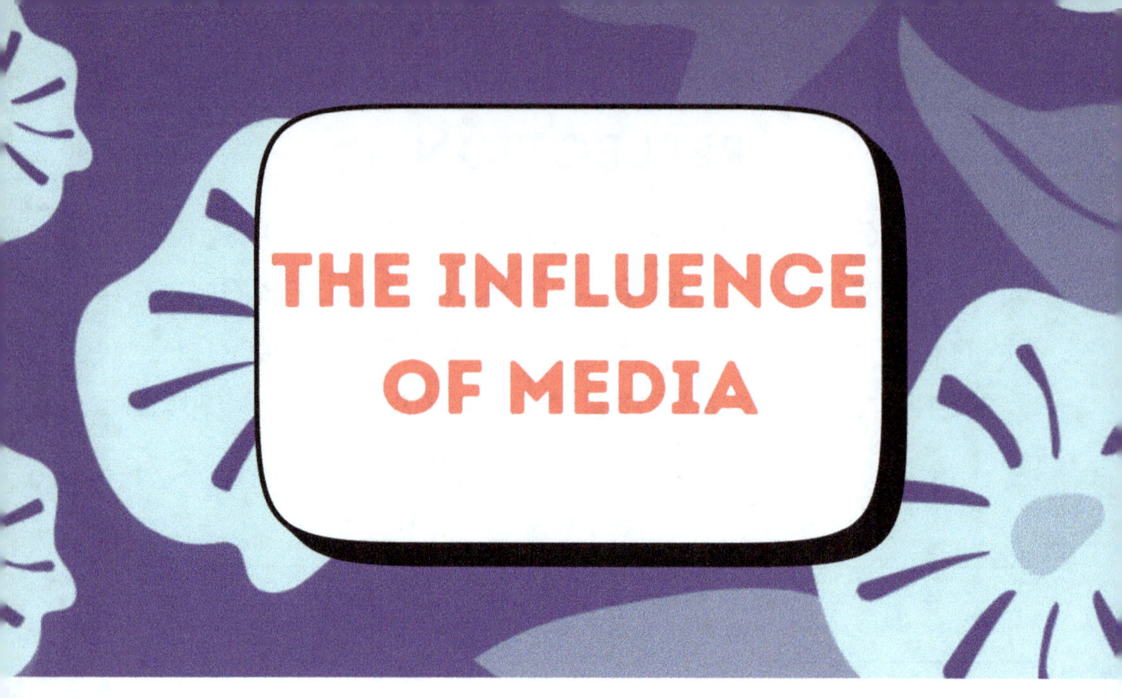

"I will not set before my eyes anything that is worthless."

Psalm 101:3

DEVOTION

True beauty and worth stem from who God made you to be, not from what you see on your screen.

REFLECTION

What messages do you absorb from the media each day, and how do they shape your view of yourself and your worth?

____

____

____

PRAYER

Dear God, help me to be mindful of the messages I consume through media. Guide me in choosing those that uplift my spirit and remind me of my true value in Your eyes.

Choose wisely what you let in, for it will shape who you become.

"But you are a chosen people, a royal priesthood, a holy nation, God's special possession, that you may declare the praises of him who called you out of darkness into his wonderful light."

1 Peter 2:9

DEVOTION

Rejection can sting, but it often redirects us to better opportunities and relationships that truly appreciate who we are.

REFLECTION

What does rejection feel like for you, and how have you seen God in those moments? How can you remember that your worth is not defined by others' opinions?

____

____

____

____

PRAYER

Dear God, when I face rejection, help me to lean into Your love and remember my true worth. Surround me with Your comfort and guide me to grow through these experiences.

Rejection is not the end; it's an opportunity for divine redirection.

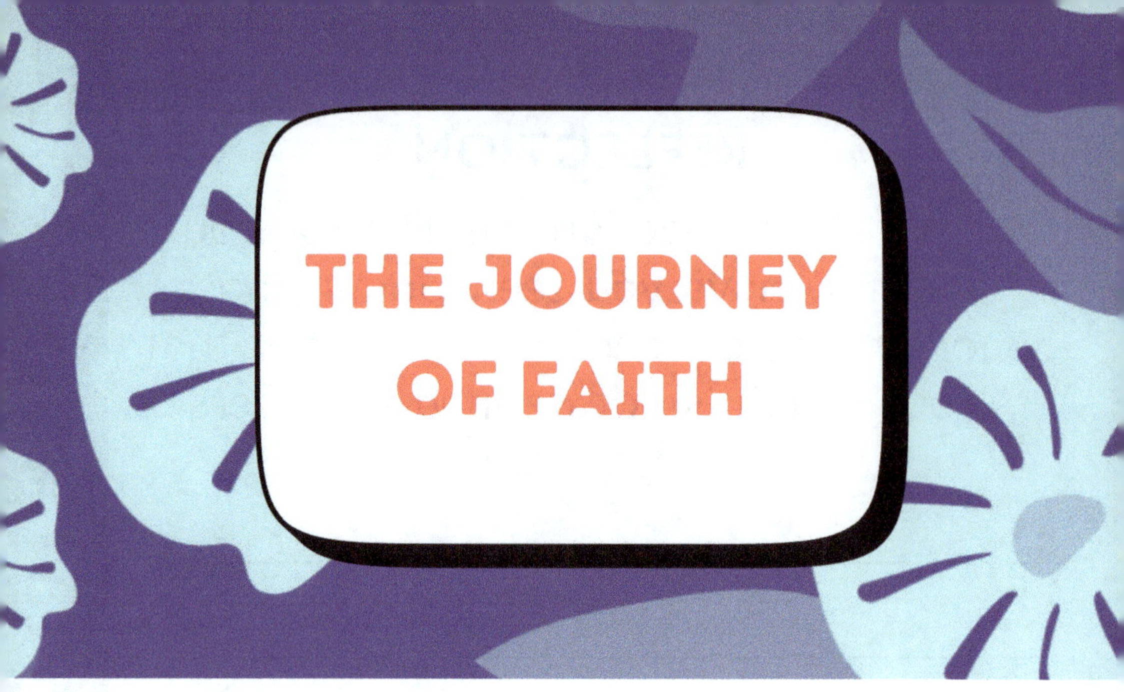

"Ask, and it will be given to you; seek, and you will find; knock, and it will be opened to you."

Matthew 7:7

DEVOTION

The path of faith is not always clear, but it is through seeking and trusting that we discover our true direction.

REFLECTION

What does your faith journey look like right now? Are there moments when you feel close to God, and others when you're searching for answers?

____

____

____

____

PRAYER

Dear God, guide me on my journey of faith. Help me to see Your presence in every step I take and to trust in Your plan for my life. Amen.

Faith is not just a destination; it's the beautiful unfolding of a story that we live each day.

"May He grant you your heart's desire
and make all your plans succeed."

Psalm 20:4

DEVOTION

Small victories are the stepping stones
that lead us toward our larger dreams,
reminding us that progress is often
made in the quieter moments of
perseverance.

REFLECTION

What small victory have you achieved recently that made you feel proud, even if it seemed minor at the time? How can you celebrate that win in a way that brings you joy?

____

____

____

____

PRAYER

Dear God, thank You for the small victories that often go unnoticed. Help me to recognize and celebrate each moment of growth in my life, big or small, and to find joy in the journey You have set before me.

Every small step forward is a leap of faith in the right direction.

"Rejoice in hope, be patient in tribulation, be constant in prayer."

Romans 12:12

DEVOTION

Faith is not just something we hold in our hearts; it's the courage to take steps, no matter how small, towards making a positive impact in the world around us.

REFLECTION

What does faith in action look like in your daily life? How can you take small steps today to show love, kindness, and trust in God to those around you?

____

____

____

____

PRAYER

Dear God, help me to live out my faith every day. Guide me as I seek to make choices that reflect Your love and grace in my life and in the lives of others.

Faith is not just a feeling; it's a choice to act in love and trust.

"In their hearts, humans plan their course, but the Lord establishes their steps."

Proverbs 16:9

DEVOTION

Trust that God's gentle nudges in your heart will lead you toward fulfilling choices that align with your true self.

REFLECTION

What decision are you facing right now
that feels overwhelming or confusing?
How can you invite God into that
process and seek His guidance?

____

____

____

____

PRAYER

Dear God, thank you for always being
by our side. Help guide us in our choices
and remind us to listen for Your voice in
our hearts.

*God's path might not always
be clear, but His presence is
always near.*

"Do everything without grumbling or arguing, so that you may become blameless and pure, "children of God without fault in a warped and crooked generation." Then you will shine among them like stars in the sky"

Philippians 2:14–15

DEVOTION

Sometimes, listening to God requires us to step away from the chaos and embrace the silence, where His guidance can be most clearly heard.

REFLECTION

How often do you take a moment to pause and truly listen for God's voice in your life? Consider the times when you felt unsure or overwhelmed—did you invite Him into those moments?

____

____

____

____

PRAYER

Dear God, help me to create space in my heart to hear Your voice. Teach me to be still and to seek Your guidance in my everyday life. Thank You for always being there to listen.

Listening to God is not about hearing His voice but recognizing His presence in the quiet moments.

"Therefore we do not lose heart. Though outwardly we are wasting away, yet inwardly we are being renewed day by day."

2 Corinthians 4:16

DEVOTION

The road to resilience is often paved with setbacks, but each challenge is an opportunity for renewal and growth.

REFLECTION

What are some challenges you've faced recently, and how did they shape your understanding of your own strength and resilience?

____

____

____

____

PRAYER

Dear God, thank You for being our source of strength and comfort. Help us to remember that resilience is a gift, and guide us to grow through our challenges, knowing we are never alone.

Resilience isn't just about bouncing back; it's about growing stronger through every storm.

"Yet, O Lord, you are our Father. We are the clay, you are the potter; we are all the work of your hand."

Isaiah 64:8

DEVOTION

Embracing your creativity can serve as an act of worship, transforming your talents into a beautiful offering that honors the Creator within you.

REFLECTION

What does creativity mean to you, and in what ways can you express your love for God through the talents and gifts you have been given?

____

____

____

____

PRAYER

Dear God, thank You for the creativity You have placed within me. Help me to see my creative expressions as a beautiful way to worship You and share Your love with the world around me. Let my art, music, or any form of creation reflect Your light.

Every brushstroke, melody, and word can be a testament to His beauty and grace

"You make known to me the path of life; you will fill me with joy in your presence, with eternal pleasures at your right hand."

Psalm 16:11

DEVOTION

Every step, no matter how difficult, holds the potential for joy and growth; remember that the journey is just as valuable as the destination.

REFLECTION

What brings you joy in your everyday life, even in the midst of challenges? Can you recall a recent experience where you found happiness despite the obstacles?

____

____

____

____

PRAYER

Dear God, help me to see the joy in every step of my journey, even when the road gets tough. Remind me that You are with me in every moment, guiding me to find light and laughter in the little things. Thank You for the gift of joy.

Joy is not found in the destination, but in the journey we take to get there.

"Rejoice always, pray continually, give thanks in all circumstances; for this is God's will for you in Christ Jesus."

1 Thessalonians 5:16–18

DEVOTION

Gratitude changes our perspective and allows us to see the beauty in our daily lives, even when things feel overwhelming or chaotic.

REFLECTION

What are the little moments in your daily life that you often overlook but can be grateful for? How can you intentionally acknowledge them today?

____

____

____

____

PRAYER

Dear God, thank you for the countless blessings in our lives. Help us to open our eyes and hearts to see the goodness around us every day.

Gratitude turns what we have into enough.

"For you created my inmost being; you knit me together in my mother's womb."

Psalm 139:13

DEVOTION

True beauty shines brightest when we embrace our authenticity, allowing others to love us for who we genuinely are.

REFLECTION

What does it look like for you to embrace your true self today, without comparing yourself to others or trying to fit into someone else's mold?

____

____

____

____

PRAYER

Dear God, help me to see myself through Your eyes, embracing the beauty and uniqueness You've created in me. May I find peace and strength in being my authentic self every day.

Authenticity is the courage to be who you really are in a world that often tells you to be someone else.

"Two are better than one, because they have a good return for their labor. If either of them falls down, one can help the other up."

Ecclesiastes 4:9-10

DEVOTION

Every friendship is a gift that teaches us the value of connection and support, reminding us that we never have to walk our journeys alone.

REFLECTION

What does friendship mean to you, and how have your friendships shaped who you are today? Can you think of a time when a friend really supported you, or when you were able to support a friend?

____

____

____

____

PRAYER

Dear God, thank You for the beautiful gift of friendship. Help me to cherish and nurture my friendships, and guide me to be a supportive friend to others.

True friendship is a treasure that enriches our lives and helps us grow.

"Wait for the Lord; be strong and take heart and wait for the Lord."

Psalm 27:14

DEVOTION

Just as flowers bloom according to their season, trust that your time will come—embracing the wait enhances our growth and shapes our future.

REFLECTION

What are some areas in your life where you find it hard to trust that God's timing is perfect? How can you lean into Him more during those moments of waiting?

____

____

____

____

PRAYER

Dear God, thank you for always being in control, even when I feel uncertain. Help me to trust in Your perfect timing and to find peace as I wait on Your plans for my life.

Waiting is not about being idle; it's about preparing for the beautiful purpose that lies ahead.

"So do not fear, for I am with you; do not be dismayed, for I am your God. I will strengthen you and help you; I will uphold you with my righteous right hand."

Isaiah 41:10

DEVOTION

Every choice we make adds to our story; failure isn't the end but a stepping stone to growth and understanding.

REFLECTION

What fears do you face when it comes to trying something new? How do these feelings hold you back from pursuing your dreams and passions?

____

____

____

____

PRAYER

Dear God, help me find courage in moments of doubt and fear. Surround me with Your love as I step forward, trusting that I am enough for every challenge ahead. Amen.

Failure is not the end, but a stepping stone toward your true greatness.

..."but those who hope in the Lord will renew their strength. They will soar on wings like eagles; they will run and not grow weary, they will walk and not be faint."

Isaiah 40:31

DEVOTION

Finding even a few moments for daily devotion can guide you into deeper faith and peace, enriching your life in ways you may never have expected.

REFLECTION

What does spending just a few moments with God each day mean to you, and how can you make that a special time for yourself?

____

____

____

____

PRAYER

Dear God, thank You for the gift of this new day. Help me to carve out time to connect with You and find joy in Your presence. Amen.

Your daily quiet time is a love letter written from your heart to God's, a space for reflection and connection.

"Whether you turn to the right or to the left, your ears will hear a voice behind you, saying, 'This is the way; walk in it.'"

Isaiah 30:21

DEVOTION

Sometimes, our life's plan unfolds in ways that we can't immediately recognize, but trusting that God has something special in store for us allows us to find peace in the journey.

REFLECTION

What are some dreams or desires you
have for your future, and how do you
think they align with God's plan for you?

____

____

____

PRAYER

Dear God, please help me to trust in
Your plan for my life. Give me clarity
and guidance as I seek to understand my
purpose and how I can best serve You.

*God's plan is a beautiful
tapestry, each thread uniquely
designed to create a
masterpiece of your life.*

"You will go out in joy and be led forth in peace; the mountains and hills will burst into song before you, and all the trees of the field will clap their hands."

Isaiah 55:12

DEVOTION

Nature shows us that life is not merely about the hustle but about stopping to appreciate the world around us, allowing joy and peace to fill our hearts.

REFLECTION

What is one way you can connect with nature this week, and how do you think it might refresh your spirit? Consider taking a moment to sit in a garden, walk in a park, or simply observe the beauty around you.

____

____

____

____

PRAYER

Dear God, thank You for the beauty of Your creation all around us. Help me to take time to enjoy and appreciate the wonders of nature, finding peace and inspiration in what You've made.

Nature is a reminder of God's artistry, inviting us to pause and reflect on His greatness.

"Therefore encourage one another and build each other up, just as in fact you are doing."

1 Thessalonians 5:11

DEVOTION

True sisterhood in Christ is about lifting each other up, creating a safe space for vulnerability, and celebrating every girl's unique journey.

REFLECTION

What does sisterhood in Christ mean to you? Think about the friendships in your life that reflect God's love and support. How can you be a better sister to those around you today?

____

____

____

____

PRAYER

Dear God, thank You for the beautiful gift of sisterhood. Help me to nurture my friendships with grace, love, and understanding, reflecting Your light in all that I do.

Sisterhood in Christ creates bonds that uplift our spirits and strengthen our faith.

"You will seek me and find me when you seek me with all your heart."

Jeremiah 29:13

DEVOTION

When we seek understanding through Scripture, we uncover not just truth, but the deeply woven fabric of our own experiences.

REFLECTION

What does the Bible mean to you personally, and how can you explore its messages as you navigate your own life's journey? Consider a story or verse that resonates with you, and why it speaks to your heart.

____

____

____

____

PRAYER

Dear God, thank you for the gift of your Word. Help me to open my heart and mind as I explore the Bible, seeking wisdom and understanding in every verse.

The Bible is not just a book; it's a love letter from God, revealing His heart and inviting you to know Him more deeply.

"Come, let us bow down in worship, let us kneel before the Lord our Maker; for he is our God and we are the people of his pasture, the flock under his care."

Psalm 95:6–7

DEVOTION

Worship is not just an act; it's a heart posture that allows us to release our burdens and embrace the joy of His presence.

REFLECTION

What does worship mean to you in your everyday life, and how can you make it a priority this week?

____

____

____

____

PRAYER

Dear God, thank you for inviting us into a beautiful relationship with You through worship. Help us to find moments each day to express our love and gratitude, drawing closer to Your heart.

Worship is not just a moment; it's a lifestyle that reflects our love for God in everything we do.

GOD'S PROMISES ARE FOR YOU

"Do not be afraid, for I am with you; I will bring your children from the east and gather you from the west. I will say to the north, 'Give them up!' and to the south, 'Do not hold them back!'"

Isaiah 43:5-6

DEVOTION

Always remember, God's promises extend to every moment of your life. Trusting in His presence allows you to face your fears and step boldly into your calling.

REFLECTION

What promises do you feel are meant for you in this moment? Can you think of a time when you experienced God's faithfulness in your life?

____

____

____

____

PRAYER

Dear God, thank you for the promises you have made to each of us. Help her to see your faithfulness in her life and to trust in your plans for her future.

God's promises are like anchors in the storms of life, holding us steady and secure.

SERVING WITH LOVE

"Serve one another humbly in love."

Galatians 5:13

DEVOTION

When we serve others with love, we uncover the incredible strength and joy that comes from genuine connection and selflessness.

REFLECTION

What does it look like for you to serve others with love in your daily life? How can small acts of kindness make a big difference in the lives of those around you?

____

____

____

____

PRAYER

Dear God, thank You for the gift of love that enables us to serve others. Help me to open my heart and hands to those in need, showing them Your kindness and compassion every day.

Serving with love transforms both the giver and the receiver.

"Being confident of this, that He who began a good work in you will carry it on to completion until the day of Christ Jesus."

Philippians 1:6

DEVOTION

Embrace your imperfections, for they are the brushstrokes of your life that create your personal masterpiece.

REFLECTION

What imperfections do you find in yourself that you could learn to appreciate and see as part of your unique beauty? How might embracing these flaws help you grow into who you're meant to be?

____

____

____

____

PRAYER

Dear God, thank you for creating me just the way I am. Help me to see the beauty in my imperfections and to embrace my journey with love and confidence.

Imperfection is not a flaw; it is the canvas of our unique beauty.

"Always be prepared to give an answer
to everyone who asks you to give the
reason for the hope that you have."

1 Peter 3:15

DEVOTION

Sharing your unique faith story can
foster deep connections and ignite hope
in others, reminding us all that our
experiences are a source of strength.

REFLECTION

What moments in your life have shaped your faith story, and how can sharing these experiences inspire those around you?

____

____

____

____

PRAYER

Dear Lord, thank You for the unique story that each of us carries. Help me to share my experiences with courage and grace, so that others may see Your love through my journey.

Your story is a thread in the beautiful tapestry of God's love.

"Jesus Christ is the same yesterday and today and forever."

Hebrews 13:8

DEVOTION

Change can be daunting, but it often leads to unexpected blessings—embracing it opens the door to becoming who you were always meant to be.

REFLECTION

What changes are you currently facing in your life, and how are you responding to them? Are you finding it easy to embrace the unknown, or do you feel hesitant?

____

____

____

____

PRAYER

Dear God, thank you for being with us through every change in our lives. Help us to embrace these moments with open hearts, trusting that you have a beautiful plan for our future. Amen.

Change is the canvas upon which our true selves can emerge.

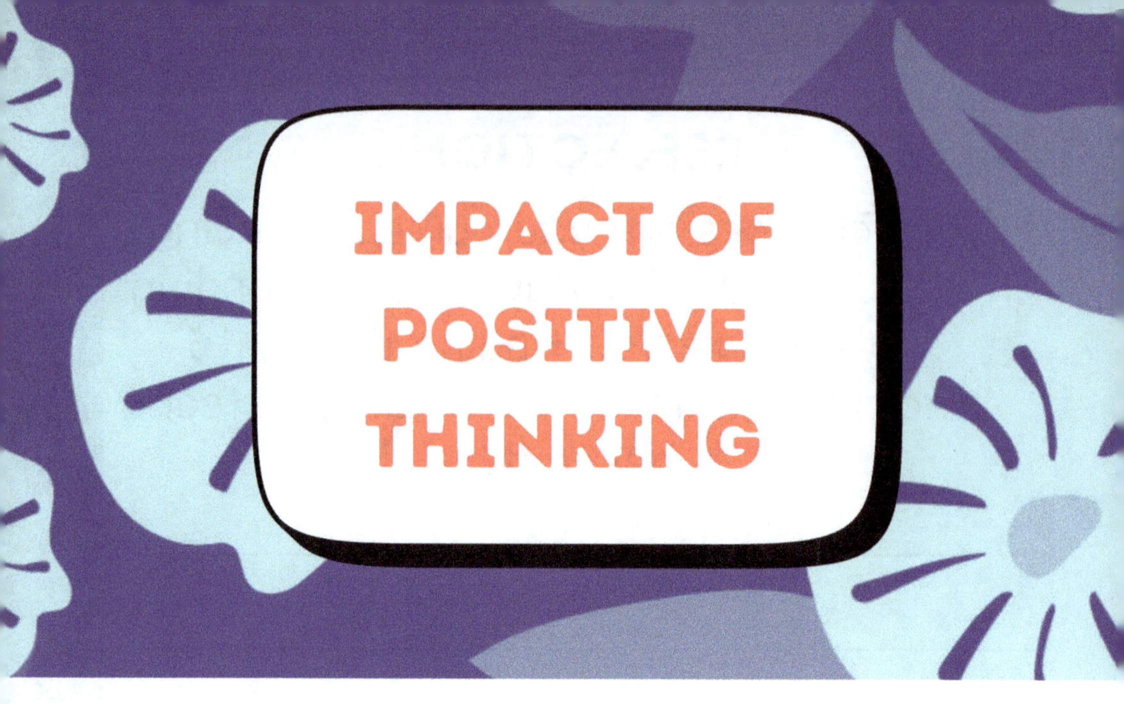

IMPACT OF POSITIVE THINKING

"Finally, brothers and sisters, whatever is true, whatever is noble, whatever is right, whatever is pure, whatever is lovely, whatever is admirable—if anything is excellent or praiseworthy—think about such things."

Philippians 4:8

DEVOTION

It's never too late to cultivate a mindset of positivity, reminding ourselves that our thoughts have the power to influence our actions and shape our lives in meaningful ways.

REFLECTION

What are some positive thoughts you can focus on today that could change how you see yourself and your world?

____

____

____

____

PRAYER

Dear God, help her to embrace the power of positive thinking. Surround her with your love and light, guiding her to see the beauty in herself and the possibilities around her. Amen.

Your thoughts shape your reality; choose them wisely.

"If any of you lacks wisdom, let him ask of God, who gives generously to all without reproach, and it will be given to him."

James 1:5

DEVOTION

Doubt is a natural part of any journey, but facing it with courage can lead to personal growth and beautiful discoveries.

REFLECTION

What doubts are you currently navigating, and how can you invite God into those moments to guide your heart toward clarity?

____

____

____

____

PRAYER

Dear God, help me remember that it's okay to question and doubt. Fill my heart with peace and clarity as I navigate through these moments, knowing that You are always walking beside me.

Even in the shadows of uncertainty, His light can guide our steps.

"Pray without ceasing."

1 Thessalonians 5:17

DEVOTION

Cultivating a prayer life isn't about finding the perfect time or place; it's about inviting God into the seemingly mundane moments of our day, creating an ongoing dialogue that nourishes our spirit.

REFLECTION

What does prayer mean to you, and how can you incorporate it into your daily life to create a deeper connection with God?

____

____

____

____

PRAYER

Dear God, thank You for always being there to listen to my heart. Help me to open up to You in prayer, finding joy and strength in our conversations. Amen.

Prayer is the quietest way to express your loudest thoughts and deepest feelings.

"Brothers and sisters, I do not consider myself yet to have taken hold of it. But one thing I do: Forgetting what is behind and straining toward what is ahead, I press on toward the goal to win the prize for which God has called me heavenward in Christ Jesus."

Philippians 3:13–14

DEVOTION

Letting go of our past empowers us to embrace the future with hope and joy, allowing God to work through us in remarkable ways.

REFLECTION

What are some things in your life that you find difficult to let go of, and how do they hold you back from experiencing peace and joy?

____

____

____

____

PRAYER

Dear God, help me to embrace the art of letting go. Fill me with Your peace as I release the burdens that weigh me down. Thank You for being my strength in this journey.

Letting go doesn't mean losing; it means making space for new blessings.

THE IMPORTANCE OF SELF-CARE

"You are precious in my sight, and honored, and I love you."

Isaiah 43:4

DEVOTION

Prioritizing self-care empowers us to not only survive but thrive, reminding us to nurture our spirit in the midst of life's demands.

REFLECTION

What does self-care mean to you, and how can you incorporate it into your daily routine to feel more balanced and whole? Consider what activities bring you joy and rejuvenation.

____

____

____

____

PRAYER

Dear God, thank you for every precious moment in our lives. Help us recognize the importance of taking care of ourselves, both physically and emotionally, so we can shine brightly in the world around us.

Embracing self-care is not selfish; it's a vital step in nurturing our true selves.

"Therefore each of you must put off falsehood and speak truthfully to your neighbor, for we are all members of one body."

Ephesians 4:25

DEVOTION

Building trust in relationships starts with being genuine; when we dare to be ourselves, we invite others to do the same.

REFLECTION

What does trust look like in your friendships, and how can you cultivate it more deeply with those around you?

____

____

____

____

PRAYER

Dear God, thank You for the relationships in our lives. Help us to build trust with others, showing love and honesty in all our interactions. May our friendships reflect Your grace and truth.

Trust is the glue that holds relationships together; without it, they can easily fall apart.

"But the Advocate, the Holy Spirit, whom the Father will send in my name, will teach you all things and will remind you of everything I have said to you."

John 14:26

DEVOTION

When we lean into the guidance of the Holy Spirit, we can navigate life's challenges with a sense of understanding and calm.

REFLECTION

What does it mean to you to have the Holy Spirit guiding your decisions and feelings in your everyday life? Can you identify moments when you felt a nudge or insight that seemed to come from within?

____

____

____

____

PRAYER

Holy Spirit, thank you for your presence in my life. Help me to listen closely to your guidance and to trust in your whispers of love and truth. May I feel your warmth leading me each day.

The Holy Spirit is the gentle whisper amidst the noise of life, always inviting you to draw closer to the heart of God.

"Commit your work to the Lord, and your plans will be established."

Proverbs 16:3

DEVOTION

Trusting God with your aspirations allows your dreams to blossom into reality in ways you might never have expected.

REFLECTION

What dreams do you hold close to your heart, and how might they align with God's greater plans for you?

____

____

____

____

PRAYER

Dear God, thank You for the dreams You've placed in my heart. Help me to believe in their potential and to trust that with You, all things are possible.

Sometimes our biggest dreams are just whispers of the incredible plans God has waiting for us.

"Consider it pure joy, my brothers and sisters, whenever you face trials of many kinds, because you know that the testing of your faith produces perseverance. Let perseverance finish its work so that you may be mature and complete, not lacking anything."

James 1:2-4

DEVOTION

Every trial is an opportunity for growth that strengthens our resolve and deepens our faith.

REFLECTION

What trials or challenges are you currently facing, and how might your faith help you grow through them?

____

____

____

____

PRAYER

Dear God, thank you for being our constant source of strength. Help this precious girl to lean on you during her trials and to find courage and hope in your promises.

Faith isn't always the absence of doubt; it's choosing to trust even when life feels uncertain.

"For just as each of us has one body with many members, and these members do not all have the same function, so in Christ we, though many, form one body, and each member belongs to all the others."

Romans 12:4–5

DEVOTION

Celebrating diversity enriches our lives and strengthens our relationships, reminding us that we are all woven together in the beautiful design of God's creation.

REFLECTION

What makes your circle of friends special? Can you think of a time when someone's unique background or perspective helped you see things differently?

____

____

____

____

PRAYER

Dear God, thank you for the beautiful tapestry of diversity in our world. Help us to appreciate each person we meet and to learn from the different experiences and stories they bring.

Embrace the differences, for they are the colors that paint the canvas of our lives.

"Whatever you do, work at it with all your heart, as working for the Lord."

Colossians 3:23

DEVOTION

Faith can be a vibrant part of a joyful life, reminding us that our beliefs can enhance our experiences and connections with others.

REFLECTION

What are some ways you can incorporate your faith into your everyday fun while staying true to yourself? Think about the activities you enjoy and how they reflect your values.

____

____

____

____

PRAYER

Dear God, help me to find joy in both my fun and my faith. May I remember that every moment can shine Your light, and I trust in Your guidance as I navigate these exciting years.

Faith can be the thread that weaves joy into the fabric of our lives.

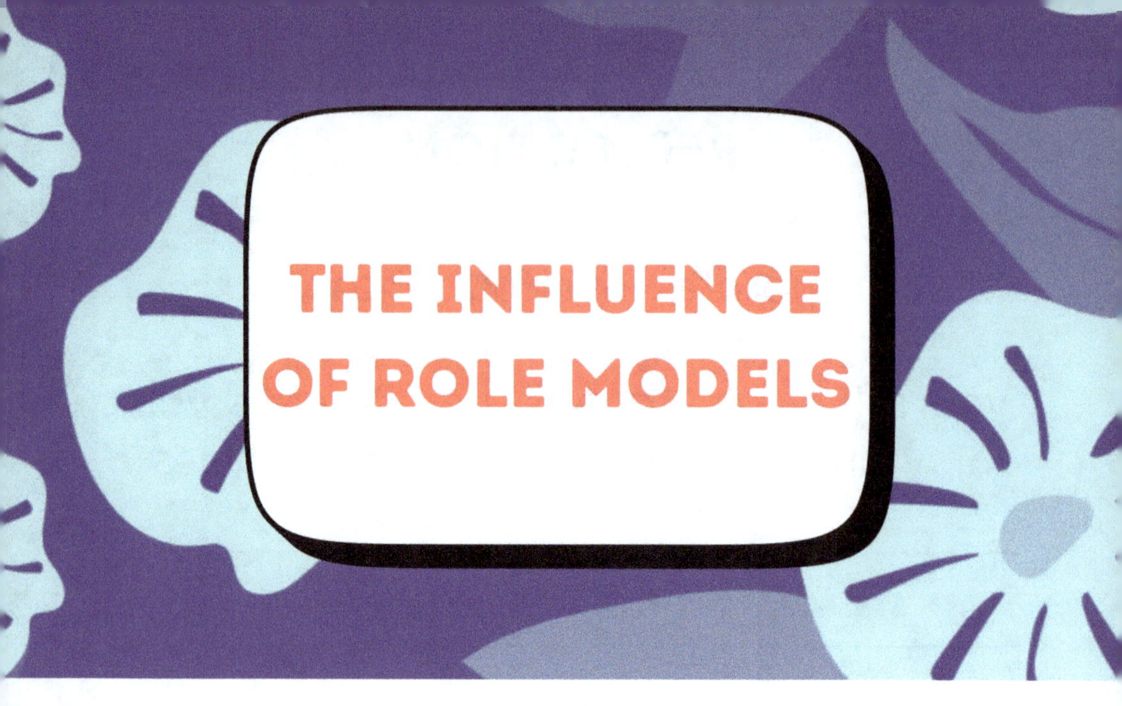

Therefore, since we are surrounded by such a great cloud of witnesses, let us throw off everything that hinders and the sin that so easily entangles. And let us run with perseverance the race marked out for us...

Hebrews 12:1

DEVOTION

Be mindful of the role models you choose, as their influence can shape the course of your journey in profound ways.

REFLECTION

What is one quality or trait you admire in someone you look up to, and how could you embody that in your own life?

____

____

____

____

PRAYER

Dear God, thank you for the role models you've placed in my life. Help me to learn from their strengths and reflect your love and light in my own actions today.

Your admiration can ignite inspiration; let it fuel your own journey.

"Behold, how good and pleasant it is when brothers dwell in unity!"

Psalm 133:1

DEVOTION

Navigating family dynamics means recognizing your own worth and expressing your voice, which can inspire others to listen and appreciate the diversity within your family.

REFLECTION

What are some specific family dynamics or relationships that challenge you the most, and how might you approach them with love and understanding?

PRAYER

Dear God, thank you for our families and the unique relationships within them. Help us to navigate our family dynamics with grace and compassion, learning to love even when it's difficult.

Navigating family dynamics takes patience, understanding, and a heart open to growth.

"The Lord is close to the brokenhearted and saves those who are crushed in spirit."

Psalm 34:18

DEVOTION

Adversity can often be the catalyst for tremendous personal growth and connection, reminding us that we can thrive even amidst struggles.

REFLECTION

What challenges are you facing right
now, and how might God be using them
to shape your character and faith?

____

____

____

____

PRAYER

Dear God, thank you for being with us
through our struggles. Help us to see
the beauty and growth that comes from
adversity in our lives. Amen.

*Every storm you survive
strengthens the roots of your
faith.*

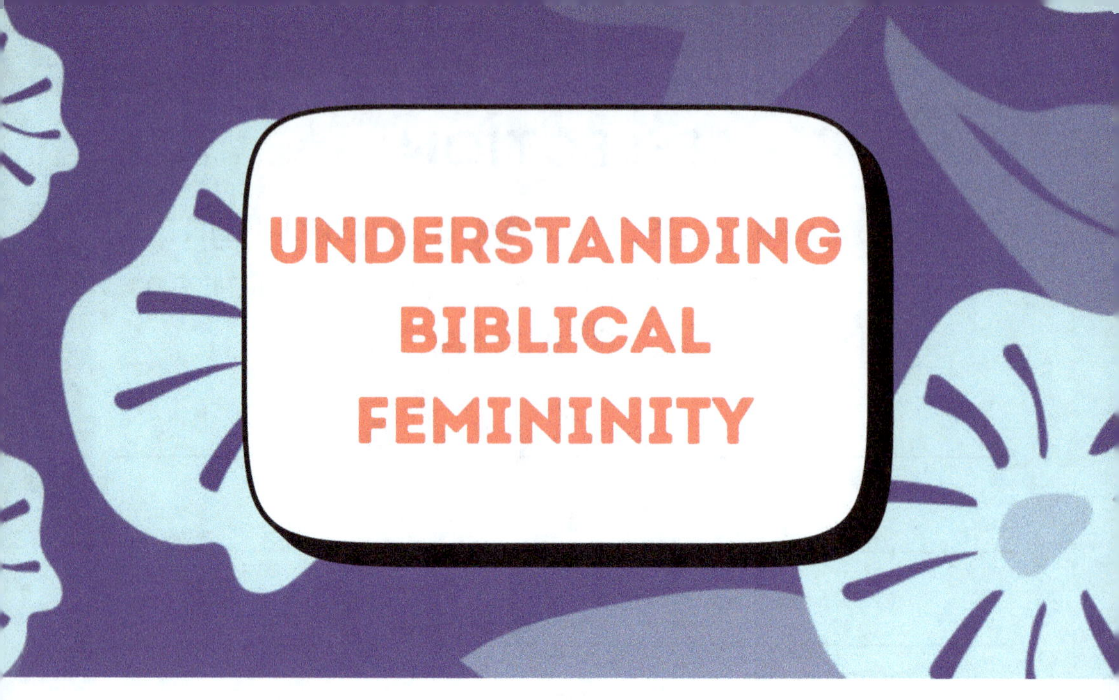

"But Ruth said, 'Do not urge me to leave you or to return from following you. For where you go, I will go, and where you lodge, I will lodge. Your people shall be my people, and your God my God. Where you die, I will die, and there will I be buried.'"

Ruth 1:16–17

DEVOTION

Embrace your distinctive journey, knowing that biblical femininity shines through acts of love and loyalty, creating a legacy simply by being true to who you are.

REFLECTION

What does it mean to you to embrace your unique identity as a girl in God's eyes? How can you celebrate the characteristics that make you uniquely feminine while staying true to your faith?

____

____

____

____

PRAYER

Dear God, thank you for creating me with purpose and beauty. Help me to understand and embrace my femininity according to your Word, and guide me to reflect your love in all I do.

True femininity is not about fitting into a mold, but about embracing the diverse ways God has created us to shine.

"I am the vine; you are the branches. If you remain in me and I in you, you will bear much fruit; apart from me you can do nothing."

John 15:5

DEVOTION

Connecting with Scripture can provide a grounding space that nurtures growth and purpose in the midst of life's demands.

REFLECTION

What does engaging with Scripture mean to you? How do you think it can shape your life and the world around you?

____

____

____

____

PRAYER

Dear God, thank you for the gift of Your Word. Help us to find joy and understanding as we read and explore its truths, guiding our hearts closer to You every day.

Scripture is not just words on a page; it's a living conversation between you and God.

"Let your gentleness be evident to all.
The Lord is near."

Philippians 4:5

DEVOTION

Contentment with what we have lays
the foundation for genuine joy and
connection in our lives.

REFLECTION

What brings you true joy in your daily
life? Can you think of moments when
you felt fully content, and what made
them special for you?

____

____

____

____

PRAYER

Dear God, thank you for the gift of
today. Help me to find joy in the little
things and to recognize your blessings
around me. Teach me to be content in
every season of my life.

*Contentment isn't having
everything; it's appreciating
what you have.*

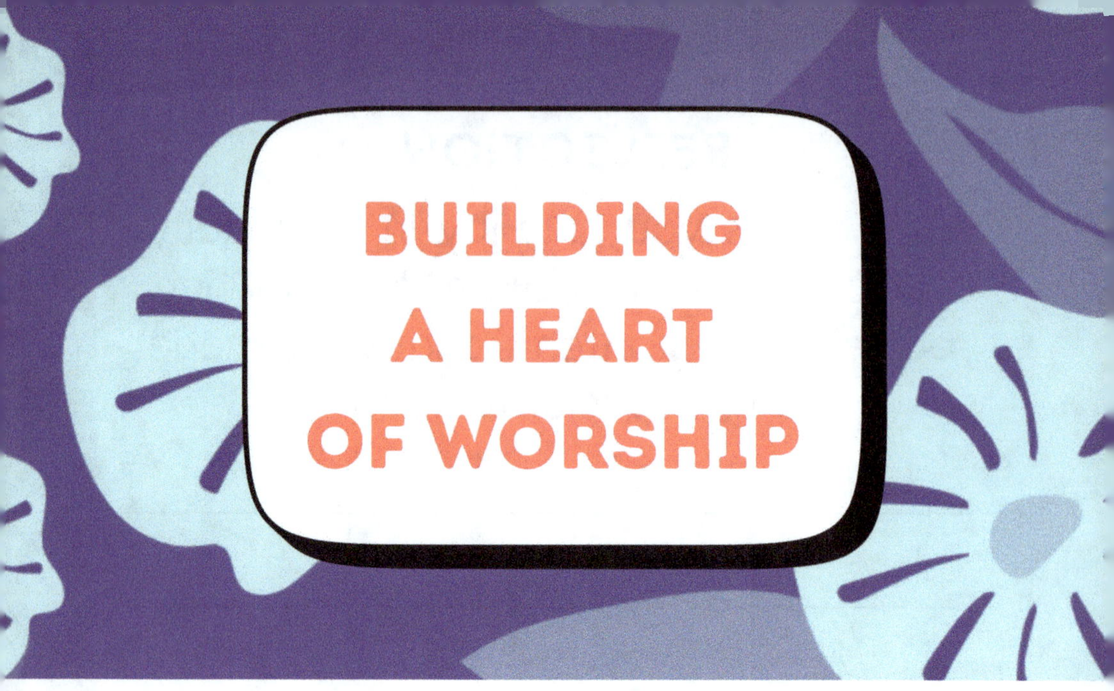

"Serve the Lord with gladness! Come into his presence with singing!"

Psalm 100:2

DEVOTION

Building a heart of worship enables us to find joy and gratitude in every aspect of our lives, no matter the challenges we face.

REFLECTION

What does worship truly mean to you?
How can you express your love for God
in your everyday life beyond singing
songs on Sunday?

____

____

____

____

PRAYER

Dear God, help me to see the beauty in
everything around me as an act of
worship. May my heart be open to
experiencing Your presence in the
simplest moments. Teach me to worship
in spirit and truth every day.

*Worship is not just a moment;
it's a lifestyle that resonates
through our actions and
words.*

"I have hidden your word in my heart
that I might not sin against you."

Psalm 119:11

DEVOTION

Staying true to your values can light a
path not just for yourself but for others
who are searching for their own way.

REFLECTION

What values are most important to you, and how do they shape your choices and interactions with those around you?

____

____

____

____

PRAYER

Dear God, help me to recognize and embrace my values in every situation I face. Guide my heart to reflect Your love and truth in my actions today.

True strength lies in living out your values, even when it's hard.

"No discipline seems pleasant at the time, but painful. Later on, however, it produces a harvest of righteousness and peace for those who have been trained by it."

Hebrews 12:11

DEVOTION

Trusting God's purposes means recognizing that our pain can lead us to unexpected blessings and growth.

REFLECTION

What is a pain or challenge you've faced that has made you question your purpose? How might trusting God in that situation change your perspective?

____

____

____

____

PRAYER

Dear God, help me to lean on you during the difficult moments. Teach me to see your purpose even when I can't understand the hurt. Fill my heart with peace and hope.

Sometimes our greatest struggles lead us to our most beautiful transformations.

THE GIFT OF ENCOURAGEMENT

"And let us consider how we may spur one another on toward love and good deeds, 25 not giving up meeting together, as some are in the habit of doing, but encouraging one another—and all the more as you see the Day approaching."

Hebrews 10:24–25

DEVOTION

Encouragement can be a profound gift we give to ourselves and others, as it fosters a deeper sense of connection and resilience.

REFLECTION

What would it look like to be the one who lifts others up with your words and actions? Can you think of a time when a kind word or gesture made a difference in your day?

____

____

____

____

PRAYER

Dear God, thank you for the gift of encouragement and for the people in our lives who inspire us. Help us to be voices of positivity and support for others, shining Your light in their moments of need.

Your words have the power to bring life to someone's spirit.

"For by grace you have been saved through faith, and that not of yourselves; it is the gift of God, not of works, lest anyone should boast."

Ephesians 2:8–9

DEVOTION

Your value is not determined by what you do or how perfectly you perform; it's rooted in the unchanging nature of God's grace that embraces you just as you are.

REFLECTION

What does it mean for you to truly embrace God's grace in times when you feel unworthy or overwhelmed by your mistakes?

____

____

____

____

PRAYER

Dear God, thank You for Your limitless grace that covers all of my shortcomings. Help me to see myself through Your eyes, embracing the love and forgiveness that You offer so freely.

Grace is not about being perfect; it's about learning to embrace our imperfections while resting in the love of a perfect God.

"Now faith is confidence in what we hope for and assurance about what we do not see."

Hebrews 11:1

DEVOTION

Faith in our relationships encourages us to choose love and truth over popularity and acceptance, leading to deeper, more meaningful connections.

REFLECTION

What does faith look like in your friendships and relationships? How do you let your beliefs guide your choices and interactions with others?

____

____

____

____

PRAYER

Dear God, thank you for the relationships you bless us with. Help me to cultivate faith in these connections, guiding me to treat others with love and understanding.

Faith in our hearts can illuminate the paths we walk together.

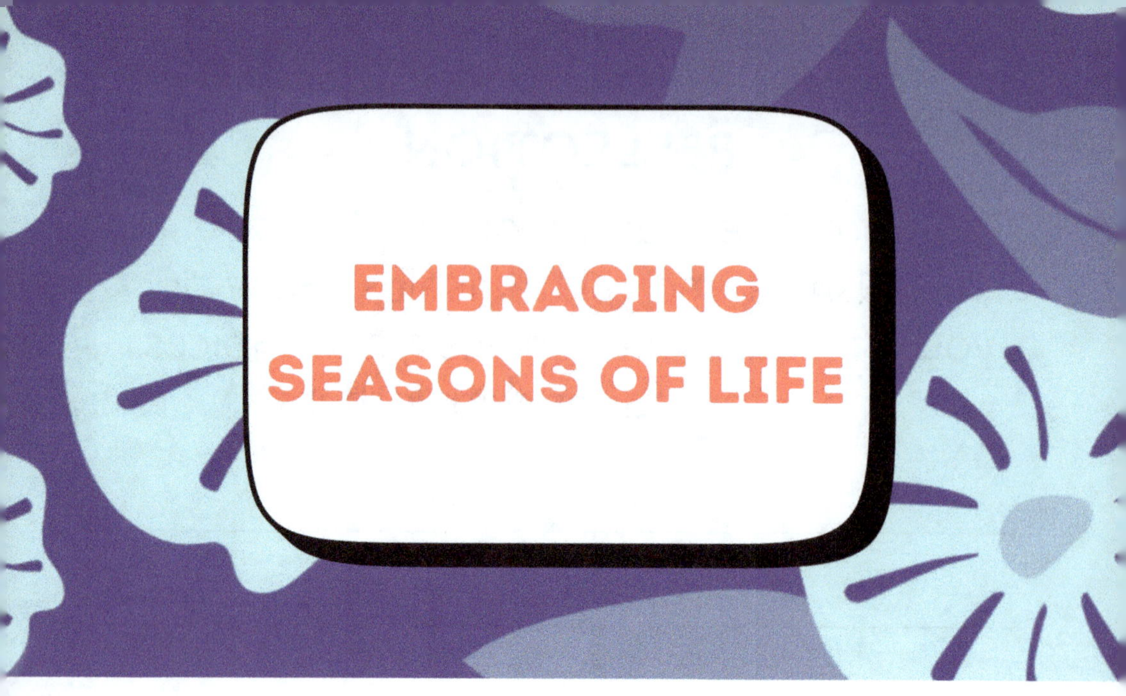

"He made the moon to mark the seasons, and the sun knows when to go down."

Psalm 104:19

DEVOTION

Embrace each season in life, for they are the foundations upon which your future blossoms.

REFLECTION

What season of life are you currently in, and how can you embrace its unique lessons and challenges?

____

____

____

____

PRAYER

Dear God, thank you for guiding me through the seasons of my life. Help me to appreciate each moment and learn from the paths I travel, knowing you are always with me.

Every season, whether bright or challenging, is a part of your beautiful journey.

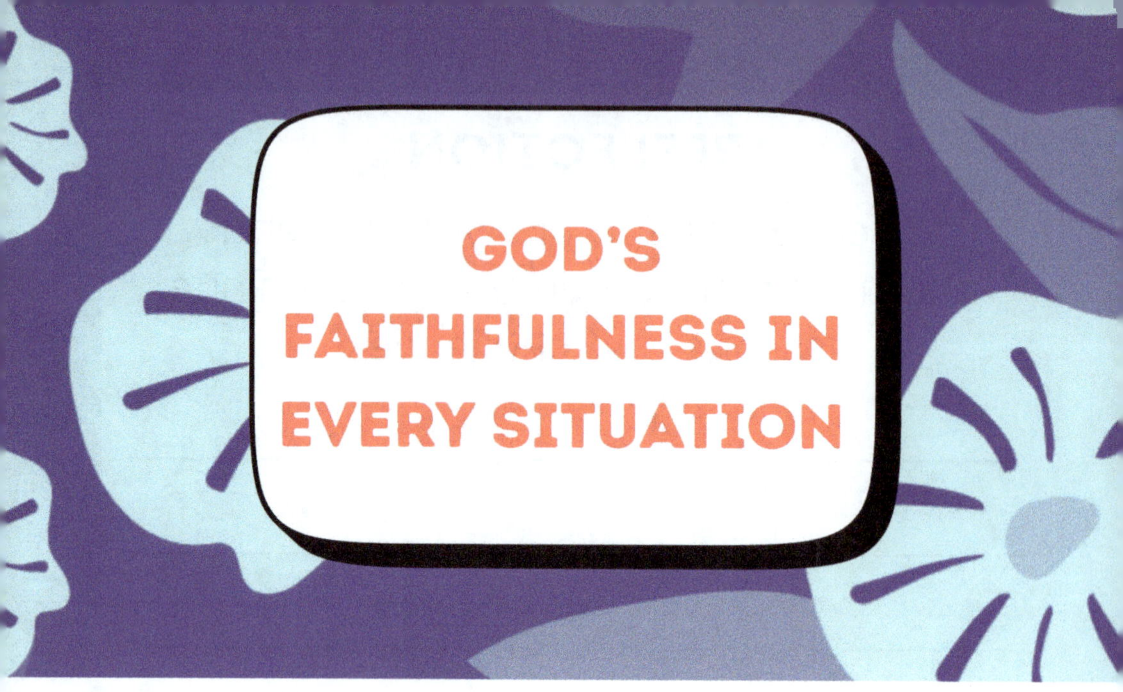

"The steadfast love of the Lord never ceases; His mercies never come to an end; they are new every morning; great is your faithfulness."

Lamentations 3:22–23

DEVOTION

God's faithfulness is like a warm blanket on a chilly night, reminding us that even in the darkest times, His love surrounds us and carries us through.

REFLECTION

What is one situation in your life right now where you need to remember God's faithfulness? How can you lean into Him during this time?

____

____

____

____

PRAYER

Dear God, thank You for being a constant source of strength and reassurance in our lives. Help us to trust in Your faithfulness, especially when we face uncertainty and challenges. Guide us to remember Your promises and find peace in Your presence.

God's faithfulness is like a lighthouse guiding us through the stormiest seas.

"My dear brothers and sisters, take note of this: Everyone should be quick to listen, slow to speak and slow to become angry,"

James 1:19

DEVOTION

Speak with kindness, for your words have the power to uplift and transform lives in ways you may never fully see.

REFLECTION

What is one kind word you can share with someone today that might brighten their day? How does it feel to be on the receiving end of encouragement and support?

____

____

____

____

PRAYER

Dear God, thank You for the gift of words. Help us to use our voices to uplift and inspire others, spreading kindness wherever we go.

Kind words can change the atmosphere of any room.

"I will not leave you as orphans; I will come to you."

John 14:18

DEVOTION

In the pursuit of overcoming loneliness, remember that reaching out to others can illuminate the path toward meaningful connections.

REFLECTION

What does loneliness feel like for you, and what are some ways you can connect with God or others during those moments?

____

____

____

____

PRAYER

Dear God, please wrap your arms around this young girl feeling lonely today. Fill her heart with the warmth of your love and the comfort of knowing she is never truly alone.

You are never alone; your heart is a part of a greater story.

"A friend loves at all times, and a brother is born for a time of adversity."

Proverbs 17:17

DEVOTION

Family moments will bloom into memories that enrich our lives. Cherish them for they are the fabric that holds us together.

REFLECTION

What is one family moment you treasure the most, and how does it remind you of the love that binds you together? Think about how you can create more of these special times.

____

____

____

____

PRAYER

Dear Lord, thank you for the gift of family. Help us to cherish every moment, finding joy in the little things and love in our connections. Amen.

Each moment shared with family is a thread that weaves the beautiful tapestry of our lives.

UNDERSTANDING FAIRNESS VS. JUSTICE

"Learn to do right; seek justice. Defend the oppressed."

Isaiah 1:17

DEVOTION

Justice is an act of compassion, showing us that it's not enough to treat everyone equally when some are in greater need of support.

REFLECTION

What does fairness mean to you in your everyday life, and how do you see it differing from justice when you encounter conflicts or make decisions?

____

____

____

____

PRAYER

Dear God, help me seek understanding in the moments I feel things are unfair. Guide my heart to act justly and embrace compassion in all situations.

Fairness is often about balance, but justice calls for deeper understanding.

"Carry each other's burdens, and in this way you will fulfill the law of Christ."

Galatians 6:2

DEVOTION

When we allow ourselves to be vulnerable and share our burdens, we deepen our connections and lighten our emotional loads.

REFLECTION

What burdens are you carrying today that you think could feel a little lighter if you shared them with a friend or trusted adult? How might opening up help both you and those you share with?

____

____

____

____

PRAYER

Dear God, help me to recognize the weight I carry and the power of sharing my burdens with others. May I find the courage to reach out and the wisdom to listen when others share theirs.

Sharing our burdens doesn't make us weak; it helps us find strength in community.

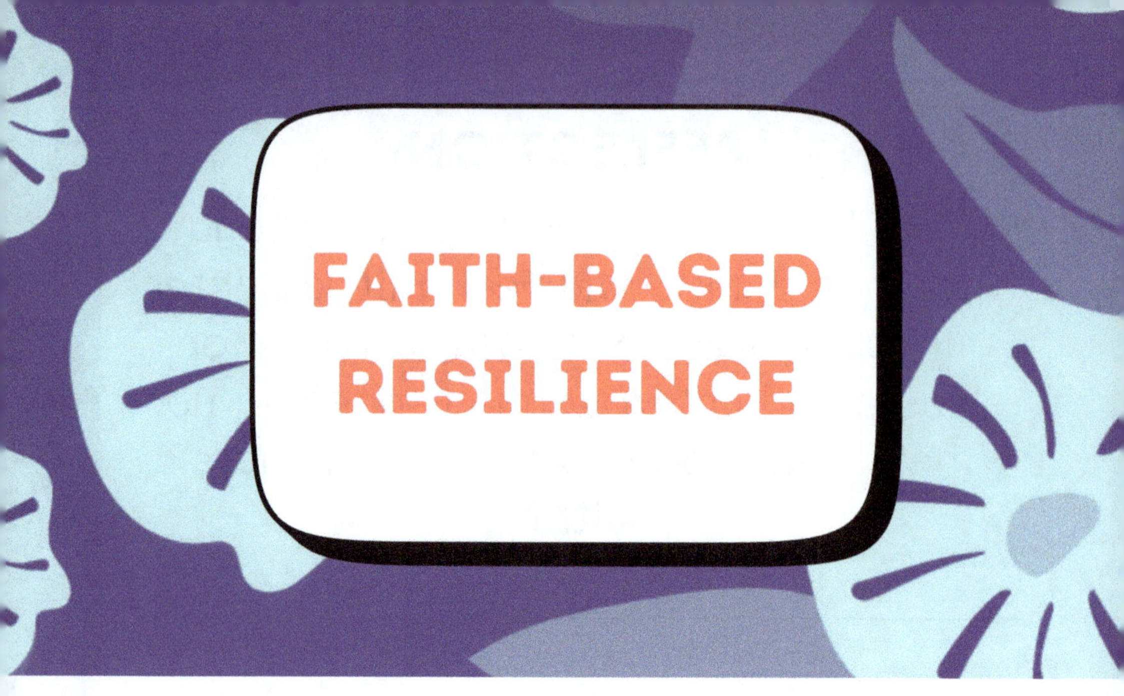

Psalm 46:1–3 reminds us that God is our refuge and strength, always ready to help in times of trouble. No matter the storms we face, whether they be small frustrations or overwhelming challenges, we can take solace knowing that we can lean on Him. In our moments of need, He stands beside us, providing calm in the chaos and the courage to rise anew.

DEVOTION

In life, resilience is not about avoiding struggles but rather about embracing them with faith and recognizing that they can lead to deeper strengths and newfound wisdom.

REFLECTION

What challenges are you currently
facing that test your faith, and how can
seeing these moments as opportunities
for growth change your perspective?

____

____

____

____

PRAYER

Dear God, thank you for being my
constant source of strength and
support. Help me to lean on You in
times of struggle and remember that
my faith can carry me through any
storm.

*Resilience is not just about
bouncing back; it's about
growing stronger through the
trials that shape us.*

THE ROLE OF SPIRITUAL MENTORING

"A student is not above his teacher, but everyone who is fully trained will be like their teacher."

Luke 6:40

DEVOTION

True spiritual mentoring blossoms when we open our hearts to share our experiences, reminding us that we grow stronger together in faith and wisdom.

REFLECTION

What does it mean to you to have someone guiding you spiritually? How can you seek out or be a mentor to someone else in your faith journey?

____

____

____

____

PRAYER

Dear God, thank You for the people You place in our lives to guide and support us. Help us to be open to learning from others and to also share our wisdom with those who seek it. Amen.

True mentoring is more than guidance; it is a tapestry of shared faith, growing together in love and understanding.

"Serve one another humbly in love, for the entire law is fulfilled in keeping this one command: 'Love your neighbor as yourself.'"

Galatians 5:13–14

DEVOTION

Serving others can lead to unexpected joys and connections that enrich our own lives.

REFLECTION

What are some ways you could use your unique gifts and talents to serve those around you, and how might that make you feel?

____

____

____

____

PRAYER

Dear God, help me open my heart to the needs of others and inspire me to take action in serving them. May my efforts reflect your love and kindness in the world. Amen.

Serving others not only uplifts them but also enriches our own lives in ways we could never imagine.

"We will not hide them from their children; we will tell the next generation the praiseworthy deeds of the Lord, His power, and the wonders He has done."

Psalm 78:4

DEVOTION

Creating a legacy of faith means actively sharing your journey and experiences with the next generation, allowing your story to be a guiding light for others.

REFLECTION

What values or beliefs do you want to pass on to those around you, and how can you start living them out today?

____

____

____

____

PRAYER

Dear God, thank You for the gift of faith that we can share with others. Help me to live in a way that inspires and nurtures those who look up to me, leaving a legacy of love and trust in You.

Faith is not just a gift; it's a legacy waiting to be shared.

"Your word is a lamp for my feet, a light on my path."

Psalm 119:105

DEVOTION

Sometimes, in the hustle and bustle of life, we simply need to pause and acknowledge the subtle signs of God's presence around us.

REFLECTION

What are some everyday moments you can pause and invite God into, even if they seem ordinary or routine? How might those moments shift for you when you focus on His presence?

____

____

____

____

PRAYER

Dear God, help us to see You in the little things today. Open our eyes to Your love and guidance in every moment we experience, big or small. Amen.

God's presence can turn the ordinary into the extraordinary.

"Show me your ways, Lord, teach me your paths. Guide me in your truth and teach me, for you are God my Savior, and my hope is in you all day long."

Psalm 25:4–5

DEVOTION

In times of confusion, remember that seeking clarity often comes through patience and trust in His divine guidance.

REFLECTION

What are some areas in your life where you feel confused right now, and how might you begin to seek clarity in those moments?

____

____

____

____

PRAYER

Dear God, as I navigate through these confusing times, help me to find peace and understanding. May Your light shine brightly in my heart and guide me on this journey. Amen.

Clarity often comes after the storm has passed; trust in the process.

"For God has not given us a spirit of fear, but of power, love, and a sound mind."

2 Timothy 1:7

DEVOTION

The choice to lean into faith rather than succumbing to fear can transform our experiences and relationships in unexpected ways.

REFLECTION

What fears are holding you back right now, and how can faith help you step beyond them?

____

____

____

____

PRAYER

Dear God, help me to trust in Your promises over my fears. Strengthen my faith so that it shines brightly in moments of doubt. May I always remember that You are with me, guiding me through every challenge.

Faith is the bridge that connects our fears to God's promises.

THE IMPORTANCE OF RESTING IN GOD

"The Lord your God is with you, the Mighty Warrior who saves. He will take great delight in you; in his love he will no longer rebuke you, but will rejoice over you with singing."

Zephaniah 3:17

DEVOTION

Resting in God is not a sign of weakness but an act of strength, reminding us to embrace His love and find renewal in His presence.

REFLECTION

What does resting in God look like for you? How can you carve out moments in your day to connect with Him and find His peace?

____

____

____

____

PRAYER

Dear God, thank you for being our safe haven. Help me to find rest in Your presence today and remind me that I am never alone in my struggles. Amen.

Resting in God is not about doing less; it's about trusting more.

"He has shown you, O mortal, what is good. And what does the Lord require of you? To act justly and to love mercy and to walk humbly with your God."

Micah 6:8

DEVOTION

In our pursuit of justice and kindness, remember that every small act of love can create ripples of transformation, both in our lives and in the lives of others.

REFLECTION

What does it mean for you to champion justice and kindness in your daily life? Are there small acts you can incorporate into your routines that reflect these values?

____

____

____

____

PRAYER

Dear God, help me to see the world through Your eyes and to extend kindness to those around me. Give me the courage to stand up for what is right and the compassion to lift others up whenever I can.

Justice and kindness are not merely actions; they are reflections of the heart.

CONQUERING SELF-DOUBT

"The thief comes only to steal and kill and destroy; I have come that they may have life, and have it to the full."

John 10:10

DEVOTION

Sometimes, we forget that even the most confident people have moments of self-doubt; it's not how we feel that defines us, but how we choose to embrace our true selves.

REFLECTION

What are the lies you believe about
yourself that hold you back from
pursuing your dreams and embracing
your unique gifts?

____

____

____

____

PRAYER

Dear God, thank You for creating me
with purpose and love. Help me to see
myself through Your eyes, overcoming
the whispers of self-doubt and
embracing my true identity. Amen.

*You are more capable and
loved than you sometimes
believe.*

"Do not lie to one another, seeing that you have put off the old self with its practices and have put on the new self, which is being renewed in knowledge after the image of its creator."

Colossians 3:9–10

DEVOTION

Stay true to who you are; the courage to embrace authenticity can inspire others to do the same.

REFLECTION

What are some lies you might be believing about yourself, and how do they conflict with the truth of who God says you are?

____

____

____

____

PRAYER

Dear God, thank You for always revealing the truth in our lives. Help me discern the lies and remind me of the beautiful truth you speak over me every day.

Truth is like a lamp – it lights the way, even in the darkest of places.

"Before I formed you in the womb, I knew you; before you were born, I set you apart..."

Jeremiah 1:5

DEVOTION

Purposeful living means understanding that your unique gifts are meant to be shared, and that your journey can inspire those around you in unexpected ways.

REFLECTION

What dreams and passions stir in your heart? How can you take small steps today to align your actions with your purpose?

____

____

____

____

PRAYER

Dear God, thank You for the unique purpose You have designed for me. Help me to listen to Your guidance and take steps in my daily life that reflect the dreams You've placed within me. Amen.

Purposeful living is not just about big dreams but also about the daily choices that reflect who we truly are.

GOD'S BEAUTY IN NATURE

"O Lord, what a variety of things you have made! In wisdom you have made them all. The earth is full of your creatures. Here is the ocean, vast and wide, teeming with life of every kind, both large and small."

Psalm 104:24–25

DEVOTION

When we pause to appreciate the beauty around us, we can see God's hand at work in both nature and our own journeys.

REFLECTION

What is one thing in nature that has recently taken your breath away, and how did it remind you of God's beauty?

____

____

____

____

PRAYER

Dear God, thank You for the beauty that surrounds us each day. Help us to see and appreciate Your creation, and let it inspire us to reflect Your love to the world.

Nature is God's way of painting the sky with hope and beauty.

"Commit your way to the Lord; trust in him, and he will do this."

Psalm 37:5

DEVOTION

Growth in faith often begins with the smallest steps, leading to profound change and renewal in our hearts.

REFLECTION

What does growing your faith look like to you right now? Are there specific areas in your life where you feel God is calling you to trust Him more deeply?

____

____

____

____

PRAYER

Dear God, thank You for being a constant source of strength and guidance in our lives. Help us to trust You more deeply and to embrace the journey of growing our faith. May we feel Your presence in every step we take.

Faith is not merely believing; it's actively trusting God in every moment.

DID THESE REFLECTIONS BRING YOU PEACE?

Hey friend,

If these Bible reflections have helped you find calm, hope, or strength when life gets overwhelming, I'd love to hear about it. Sharing your review on Amazon can help other teen girls—just like you—discover moments of comfort when they need it most.

To leave your thoughts, simply scan the QR code below or enter the link in your browser.
Your words could be exactly what someone else needs today.

https://go.binnovatedigital.com/teengirlsbible

www.ingramcontent.com/pod-product-compliance
Lightning Source LLC
Chambersburg PA
CBHW050817070726
47592CB00030B/745